T0129319

A Coconut's Reflections

*a.k.a. A present-day reflection
of yesteryear's sketches*

Willie G(arcia)

authorHOUSE®

AuthorHouse™
1663 Liberty Drive
Bloomington, IN 47403
www.authorhouse.com
Phone: 1 (800) 839-8640

Published by AuthorHouse 06/12/2018

ISBN: 978-1-5462-4626-8 (sc)
ISBN: 978-1-5462-4624-4 (hc)
ISBN: 978-1-5462-4625-1 (e)

Library of Congress Control Number: 2018906855

Print information available on the last page.

Any people depicted in stock imagery provided by Getty Images are models, and such images are being used for illustrative purposes only. Certain stock imagery © Getty Images.

This book is printed on acid-free paper.

Because of the dynamic nature of the Internet, any web addresses or links contained in this book may have changed since publication and may no longer be valid. The views expressed in this work are solely those of the author and do not necessarily reflect the views of the publisher, and the publisher hereby disclaims any responsibility for them.

Acknowledgement

I would like to acknowledge a few individuals that have aided in my authorship of this collection. First, I would like to thank my initial critics who were asked to review, critique and provide the necessary criticism in hopes of increasing my readership to the next level. In the area of inspiration or influence, I, definitely, have to give special thanks to the following individuals: my aunt Lydia - a family writer; Cyntia who was my co-editor during my earlier years as a high school yearbook advisor and initially introduced me to "mandoize stories"; my cousin Marissa a high school newspaper writer; two close friends, Cynthia and Jazmin (Bertha), who allowed me to listen to their life histories and interpret their feelings into a majority of my writings; Gabriela & Vero(nica) who made me view things from so many different angles; my high school classmates Linda and Dorothy (Dot), who unknowingly raised my awareness of the world around me. I, also, would like to thank my son, Nicholas for constantly pushing me to write my story. In closing, I would like to thank three special individuals that have guided me, Nicholas and Ofelia, my parents as well as my Mama-Tia Gila. My parents have both passed on, but they continue to be an influence on me. As for my Mama-Tia Gila, I love you for all that you have done and continue to do for me.

Preface

This collection is based on the hardships that students endured, in their short lives, prior to entering my classroom. In addition, they are the empathetic understanding, of the author, as he listened to the words of others. To these I have kept my promise to not identify you but unfold your stories through my poetic interpretation.

Age

Age, a number, an alternative
A time tool to measure
Or passage
Some return to days gone by
Others mature and wither 'way
Ignored, others ridicule and laugh
While some capture and elate
Age a preference, age a choice

Ain't Enuf

Feeling, caring, knowing
Ain't enuf . . .
B.F.F'n it
Ain't enuf . . .
Family, a home, a shelter
Ain't enuf . . .
Blood making families
Ain't enuf . . .
'member
Ain't enuf . . .
"Sorry, sorry, sorry"
Ain't enuf . . .
Love defin'n us
Ain't enuf . . .
Me belonging to you
You belonging to me
Is . . .

Ain't No Comin' Back...

Released from her loins
I wasn't going back
Comforted and nurtured
I wasn't going back
Cultured and raised
I wasn't going back
Educated and socialized
I wasn't going back
Trained and invested
I wasn't going back
Passing time
I wasn't going back
No ills, no bills
I wasn't going back
Soaring high or crashing down
I wasn't coming back

America's Flag

We live and die by it
Why?
To be stepped on,
Spat on,
Ignored
Set on fire,
Or called second class
Not mine,
At least not mine
Yet, ignorance rules
Yet, choices influence actions
Yet, it's here where I chose to be
To speak one's mind
To express one's self,
Even protesting at our nation's steps.
It's here where I am F R E E
Here
Here by OUR flag

Appreciation

Effective evolution
Succeeding processes, ignoring failures
Securing individuality and creativity
Surfacing mutations
Removing normalcy
Removing life
Its memory
Its misery
Its beauty
Capturing its happiness
Capturing the soul
Capturing the spirit
Knowing you
Knowing me
Knowing me
Knowing you
Releasing me
Releasing you
Appreciation

Blocked and Untouched...

It was an age of enlightenment
Blocked and untouched . . .
Creating character and flaws
Growing in maturity or in neglect
Blocked and untouched . . .
Raising ignorance or thought
Animating movement and freedom
Blocked and untouched . . .
Pursuing gains and advances
Through the challenges of the superiors, inferiors or peers
Blocked and untouched . . .
Yet lost in a World of Ups and Down
This Age of Consent
Blocked and untouched . . .

Brothers & Sisters

Made from unconditional love
I am a child with purpose
Playing, laughing, and crying
I am a child with purpose
Rising to survive
I am a child with purpose
Birthing Baby Boomers, Love – Peace, & Generation X
I am a child with purpose
Remaining members of the Greatest Generation
I am a child with purpose
Repenting and forgiving brothers and sisters
I am a child with purpose
Kati, Ofelia, Lydia, Gila, Fidel, Ismael, Gloria, Xochitl & Frank
I am a child with purpose

Centered

So many roads untraveled
So many riddles unsolved
Bewildered, confused or puzzled
I am centered
Socially, emotionally, or academically
I will not settle for less
I am centered
Responsible and rounded
I am centered
Encouraged rather than discouraged
I will continue
To be centered

Challenges

So many wrongs
So few rights
Ashamed of what I've done
Maybe yes? Maybe no?
Always a part of me
A page never turned
A book never closed
The rose unfinished
Always a memory
Always a dream

Children of Candor...

A youthful word
A childish smile
And an OMG in disbelief
Being obscured and sincere
These babes cried out
Energized and spirited
"I pledge allegiance . . ." and ". . . land of liberty . . ."
Forming influential & impressionable minds
These children of candor, of innocence
Compromising our standards
Agreeing on their stares
Or awaiting their glares

Communicate

Respect vs trust vs love
Communicate - Communication . . .
Fascination vs joy vs laughter
Communicate - Communication . . .
Sadness vs emotion vs death
Communicate - Communication . . .
Self-reliance vs memory vs art
Communicate - Communication . . .
Intensity vs anger vs maturity
Communicate - Communication . . .
Child vs adolescence vs adulthood
Communicate - Communication . . .

Confused

No puedo (no, I can't)
si, si puede (yes, it can be done)
What words
What power
What an impact
Yet ignored
Yet misunderstood
Y siempre confundido (and always confused)

Connections...

Channeling days, weeks, & months
Decorated with pain
Bred, blossomed or nurtured
Gripping maturity & irresponsibility
Fueled with emotion
Riding sunrises & sunsets
For you, for me, for us . . .

Cross – Road Orphan

I turn and heard a cry
Safety cradled inches away
Then, there was a cry
He, God, had done no wrong
Then, there was a cry
I was on my way
Then, there was a cry
Fighting silently amongst themselves
Then, there was a cry
Leaving insecurity at its beckoning call
Then, there was a cry
United then divided
Then, there was a cry
I had erred leaving broken
Then, there was a cry
"Be careful", "Be a guiding light"
Then, there was a cry
Aged silence withered reason
Then, there was a cry
Reluctance held on

Then, there was a cry
Now, there is neither
Then, there was a cry
Another 'orphan by death'
Then, there was a cry
Losing those called Mother and Father

Cuando vez estos ojos...

(when you see these eyes)

Different but same
Cuando vez estos ojos . . .
To see that smile
Cuando vez estos ojos . . .
To see those eyes
Crazy, you saving me
Cuando vez estos ojos . . .
Skipping hearts, skipping beats
Cuando vez estos ojos . . .
Kiss'n eyes, kiss'n lips
Chang'n life, chang'n mine
Cuando vez estos ojos . . .
Don't leave me
Cuando vez estos ojos . . .
Happiness found flying around
Seeing those eyes
Cuando vez estos ojos . . .

Damaged Prejudice

She wished
For this & that
Joy, happiness, or love
Shattered with
Abuse, injury & ridicule
Some yelled HO!
She claimed SURVIVAL
Other stated IGNORANCE
She echoed, WE ALL SEEK REWARD!!!
Monetary, Socially, Emotionally, or Physically
Compromising ourselves
Prostituting one another

Days of Future Past

Responding with echoed "Present", "Late", or "Not Here"
Days of future past . . .
Seeing chaotic discipline or bias competition
Days of future past . . .
Confronting to rigid schedules, appointments or commitments
Days of future past . . .
Promises were given, kept or broken
Days of future past . . .
Valued clues, claims and choices
Days of future past . . .
Revealing lessons being taught or learned
Days of future past . . .
Achieving desired dreams and desired goals
Days of future . . . *Days of* past. . .
Days of future past . . .

D & A...

Deserted and abandoned
I was without
A friend, a heart, a soul
I was without
Divorced, separated, removed
I was without
Tearing and unwavering
I was without
Returning one day
I remained without
Deserted and abandoned
A love found
A truth made & seen

Deepest Fear

(Unrecognized)

Individual inadequacies
Unrecognized undefined . . .
Unmeasurable power
Unrecognized undefined . . .
Illuminating fear over frightened darkness
Unrecognized undefined . . .
Humility over arrogance and conceit
Unrecognized undefined . . .
Acceptance over concealed talent
Unrecognized undefined . . .
Liberated fear and followers
Unrecognized undefined . . .
Insecurities
Recognized, recognized, recognized . . .

Defeated & Retreated

Sin palabras (without words)
I had failed
Or had they
Si se puede (Yes, it can be done)
Words without meaning
Words without strength
They were just words
Echoed sentiments of long ago
Replaced by the futility
And why, why, why

Dejected & Rejected

Lookin' in
Ignored and unrecognized
Lookin' in
An obscured phantom
Lookin' in
Humiliated, bullied, and scarred
Lookin' in
Hooded shadows, carved ugliness
Lookin' in
Jealousy and conceit
Lookin' in
Bullied and unchallenged
Lookin' in

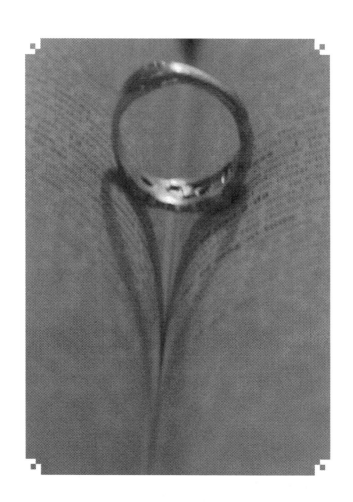

Delusion of an Illusion

Was it a need, a want, a desire
Meeting resistance or hesitation
Reaching out for comfort and counsel
Turning a dream into a reality
Rather than illusion
This fantasy
This hope
This shattered dream
This delusion of an illusion
To touch
To hold
To love

Destiny

Each soul creating one
Molding minds
To question
To THINK
Touching them
Opening walkable doors
Venturing a thousand-mile journey
Choosing roads, drives, streets and avenues
Succeeding where others had not
Destiny

Disputed...

I did it
Me, myself, and I
Removing stigmas
Me, myself, and I
Humiliated and ignored
I did it – Me, myself, and I
Wrong or right
I did it – Me, myself, and I
Scared or scarred
I did it – Me, myself, and I
Removing the riches
I did it – Me, myself, and I
Success
Mine
Me, myself, and I

Don't ever look back...

To persuade, influence, or ignore
Don't ever look back . . .
Believing and feeling,
Being ONE not two, three nor four
Don't ever look back . . .
Entering the night and finding light
Don't ever look back . . .
Connecting letters, words, ideas
Don't ever look back . . .
Revealing windows
Souls, emotions, love, hate or despair
Don't every look back . . .
Comforting arms
Warmth, safety and security
Don't ever look back . . .
Amazing character, beautiful persona
Don't ever look back . . .

Dream Chaser Catcher

Visionary fantasy
Desired goal
Chaser catcher
Ventures quest
Arduous destiny
Chaser catcher
Destructive production
Eliminated creation
Chaser catcher
Emotional sensation
Accepted declination
Chaser catcher

Egging others and another

Trying
Prevailing
Creating
Seeking
Attempting conquests
Settling for mediocrity
Reaching the attainable
Reaching the un…
Believing
Scoffing
When said and done
Questioned fortune
Finding failures
Finding S-u-c-c-e-s-s

Eluding – Part One

Strangers passing
Boats colliding
Ships eluding
Tranquil peace
Silent waters
Fiery beauty
Unforgiven revelations
Blinded journey
Unanswered queries
Transparent visions
Visible markers
One step forward
One step back

Erupt, explode...

Careless callous
Reckless abandon
Erupt, explode . . .
Disturb, burst, collapse
Erupt, explode . . .
Bruises, cuts and death
Erupt, explode . . .
Disregarding compassion
Erupt, explode . . .
Gathering anger, revenge, violence
Erupt, explode . . .
Leaving destruction
Erupt, explode . . .

Fantasies & Visions

Clarity raised blindness
Challenges created ignorance
Wonderment produced chase
Humility satisfied arrogance
Dreams beckoned desires
Fantasies & Visions
Visions & Fantasies

Fragile is the I

Held by stressors
Good or bad
Withered by time
Disillusioned by many
Held together by few
Recalling the worse
Rather than the best
Ending in distrust
Emotional anger
Disharmony & displeasure

Friends

Passing time
Friends or colleagues
Coming and going
Colleagues or associates
Promising or uncommitting
Associates or acquaintances
Passing hellos and goodbyes
Friends or acquaintances
Fade, faded, fading
F r i e n d s

Frozen in Time

A, "Will you start?"
"Who's paying", follows
"You pay"," I pay", "Split?"
Frozen in time
Gimme, gimme, gimme
A yes, a no, a can't, a won't
Frozen in time
Envied attire
The glance
Up, down
Down, up
Smiling selfies
Frozen in time
Going 'our' ways,
Ladies or gents
Grinding or twerking
Playing video B-ball
Ignoring meals, ladies, and nights
Frozen in time
Ending moments
Frozen in time
Memories to 'member
Memories to forget
Frozen in time

Gestures

Movements, shrugs and looks
Gestures . . .
Hands to mouth
Mouth to hands
Gestures . . .
Eyes to lips
Lips to eyes
Gestures . . .
A word whispered
A word exploded
Gestures . . .
Touching me
Touching you
Gestures . . .

Gone...

Days gone . . .
Family respect
Surfaced selfishness
Days gone . . .
Following authority
Surfacing defiance
Days gone . . .
Freedom rings
Surfacing revolution
Days gone . . .
Where right is right
Surfacing chaos
Days gone . . .
Thriving competition
Surfacing involved equality

Gurllllll – You're Baddddddd NO!!!! You're Gooood

a.k.a. What to do . . .

What to do . . .
NEEDING discipline & rules
ASKING love and acceptance
What to do . . .
Curbing authority and respect
FIGHTING permission or forgiveness
What to do . . .
REVEALING discomfort and pain
FEELINGS shared or experienced
What to do . . .
FINDING destiny's choices or values
ASKING justice or equality
What to do . . . What to do . . .

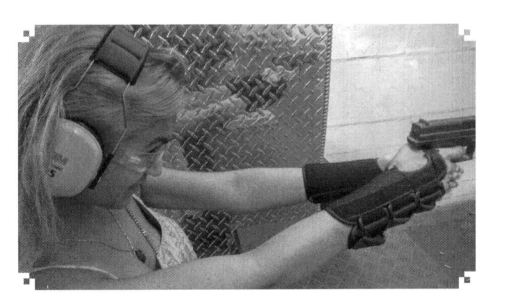

He Calls

Providing *CHOICE*
He calls . . .
Embracing *TRUST*
He calls . . .
Rejoiced *FULFILLMENT*
He calls . . .
Through *RHYME, VERSE* and *SPIRIT*
He calls . . .
Providing *GLORY* and *PRAISE*
He calls . . .
The *CREATOR of FAITH*
He calls . . .
The *SAVIOR* of *MAN*
He calls . . .

He Saw... He Tried...

When he saw wrong
He tried to right it
When he saw drama
He tried to leave it
When he saw evil
He tried to reverse it
When he saw hate
He tried to remove it
When he saw chaos
He tried peace
When he saw uncertainty
He tried charity, compassion and comfort
When He Saw . . . He Tried

Hidden...

. . . *AGENDAS*
destruction . . .
GLORIFIED WARS
destruction . . .
STRATEGIC EXITS
destruction . . .
FALLEN SOULS AND LIMBS
utter chaos . . .
RELINQUISHING DARKNESS AND DEMONS
wars, cheers and tears
HIDDEN . . .
. . . agendas

His Image

Time's re-creation
His image . . .
Life's definition
His image . . .
Journey's turns
His image . . .
Positions assigned if not created
His image . . .
Destiny's appointment
His image . . .
Struggling weaknesses
His image . . .
Strengthening faith
His image . . .
Glorified
His image . . .
Robing love
His image . . .
Redeeming chaotic failures
His image . . .
Self-centered and judgmental
His image . . .
Followed, followed, followed
His image . . .

His Purpose

Adopted son
His purpose . . .
Disciplined brotherhood
His purpose . . .
Changing lives
His purpose . . .
A willingness
His purpose . . .
Another day another night
His purpose . . .
Bridging lives
His purpose . . .
The willing path
His purpose . . .
Its turns, dips, and bruises
His purpose . . .

Hug Me

No weakness
Hug me
No dependency
Hug me
It's affection
Hug me
It's respect
It's admiration
DAMN IT!! JUST HUG ME!!
It's love

I Am . . . character

I AM **Strong, Brave, & Smart**
FOR I AM AMBITIOUS, CONFIDENT, & CAPABLE
I AM **Generous, Benevolent, & Protective**
FOR I AM DETERMINED, EXCLUSIVE & PROUD
I AM **Talented, Tough, & Vivacious**
FOR I KNOW WHAT I WANT
I AM **Independent, Hardworking, & Determined**
FOR NOTHING WILL DETER ME
I AM **<u>Vero(nica)</u>**

I Am . . . ed

I am balanced and centered
I am . . .
Inspired and respected
I am . . .
Directed and oriented
I am . . .
Nurtured and bewildered
I am . . .
Encouraged and believed
I am . . . loved
I am . . . I am

I Am No One

Good, bad, or indifferent
Man, woman, or child
I am no one
Giving birth, food, shelter, clothes and love
Providing guidance care and discipline
I am no one
Allowances provided
Patience grew
I am no one
Discipline reflects kindness, smiles, and joy
Actions left laughter, tears, and anger
I am no one
Life cares not for wants or needs
These memories will live
For I am not alone
I was and am cherished
I was and am embraced

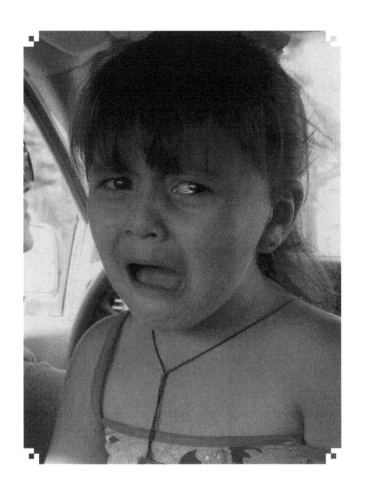

I cried a little...

In darkest times
I cried a little
Even comforted and consoled
I cried a little
Speaking charismatically and truthfully
I cried a little
Displaying pride and respect
I cried a little
With your continuous love and beauty
I cried a little
With your waning pain and shining heart
I cried a little
Your passage created my emptiness
I cried a little
Yesterday, today and tomorrow
I cried a little

If I Had...

A day to give you
I WOULD . . .
GIVE a shoulder to LEAN on
Give an arm to EMBRACE
Give a hand to LIFT
IF I HAD
A day to give you
I WOULD . . .
Shed a tear of joy, happiness or sorrow
WITH SOFTEN LIPS, SMILE WIDE,
Smile BRIGHT and smile BIG
WITH A GENTLE TONGUE WHETHER
RICH OR POOR
SPEAK of dreams, goals, and futures
IF, IF I HAD . . .
I WOULD . . . I WOULD . . .

If only...

I could, I would
If only . . .
Go back in time
If only . . .
I wouldn't waver
If only . . .
I'd sweep
If only . . .
I'd bedazzle and dazzle
If only . . .
I'd adore and adorn
If only . . .
I'd relish
I'd care
I'd provide
Shelter and protect
If only . . .

Ignition On...

Harmony and discord embrace the floor
Pretenders play on
Once upon a time
Magic, mystery, spells
It goes on and on . . .
Freezing sound, speed or time
Seizing the moment, hammering regrets
Breaking chains, breaking bondage
Igniting fire, hopes and dreams

In Me

This is me – not you
Endless possibilities – in me
Reaching in or out – but meddling
Endless possibilities – in me
One can – with mischief
One can – with playful curiosity
Visualize - endless possibilities
Endless possibilities – in me
Without words - memories, voices, & times
Endless possibilities – in me

Inner Portals

She told me to believe
He told me to fail
Entries, gateways, thresholds
Continued confusion
Ignoring translations
Entries, gateways, thresholds
Avoiding confrontations
Fearful errors
Entries, gateways, thresholds
Doubting reactions
Welcoming approvals
Entries, gateways, thresholds
Realizing interpretations
Failures successes
Entries, gateways, thresholds
Inner portals . . .
Entries, gateways, thresholds

Inner Sanctuary

We retreat
Child, adolescent, or adult
Entering memories fond or unkind
We retreat
Crossing paths with friends, foes or the unknown
Resisting if not creating temptation through words or acts
We retreat
Knowing or 'un' the unexpected becomes
We retreat
Into the INNER SANCTUARY
We retreat

It's My Way...

He said, she said
It doesn't matter
IT'S MY WAY...
Go straight, go back
No, I want left, **No, right**
IT'S MY WAY...
Didn't understand, too bad
What I want! *I get!*
'Cuz I can manipulate
IT'S MY WAY...
It's the Only Way
And there ain't no shame

Legacy...

I believe - I am who I am
Through no fault of mine
Beaten, scarred or abused – I survived
Through no fault of mine
Ignored, betrayed and unloved
Through no fault of mine
Sheltered, hidden & denied
Through no fault of mine
I have succeeded where stronger have failed
Through no fault of mine
Legacy . . .

Life's Highways

Finding **structure**
Finding **purpose**
Finding doors **opened** *or* **closed**
Raising questions
What to do ???
When to venture ???
Or *why me ???*
Raising answers
Because,
Why not
Raising hopes
Finding MISSED OPPORTUNITIES
CRUSHING DREAMS
Life's roads
Life's streets
Life's highways

Little Voices

Why?
You scared me!!!
Liking this room
Little Voices . . .
While Johnny B. Good
Having fun
Little Voices . . .
Wah!, Wah!!, Wah!!!, book buddies
One story, then the next
Attentive, wandering,
Listening, ignoring
Little Voices . . .
The child remains within
Reading classics, fiction or fact
Little Voices . . .
And gaming Rescue the Fish, Shoots & Ladders or Candyland
Little Voices . . .

Look Around

I'm a BIGGGG girl now
Look around . . .
I'm on my own
Look around . . .
I'm young not old
Look around . . .
Let me be me
Look around . . .
Challenged and I'll put you down
Look around . . .
Treat me equal
Look around . . .
I KNOW, I'M RIGHT
Look around . . .
You WERE here but NEVER HERE
Look around . . .
I'm hurt, confused, and disturbed
Look around . . .
I cry HELP and YOU TURN
Look around . . .
SEE ME, SEE YOU
Look around . . .
SEE YOU SEE ME
Look around . . .
Look around . . .

Lost souls

First glance, desires, dreams & goals
I'll never be with you
Rejection, pain, revenge, or hate
I'll never be with you
Passing opportunities, emotional ties
I'll never be with you
To touch, dance, and love again
I'll never be with you
Never you

The Man I Love...

Dance with Me
The Man I Love
Work with Me
The Man I love
Play with Me
The Man I Love
Pray with Me
The Man I Love
Lay with Me
The Man I Love
Be One with Me
The Man I Love
I Miss You
The Man I Love

Me, Myself and I

I STAND SEARCHING
BUT I STAND KNOWING
I STAND EXPECTING
BUT I STAND CONFIDENT
I STAND TOLERANT
BUT I STAND ACCEPTING
I STAND CONFUSED
BUT I STAND ENLIGHTENED
I STAND ABANDONED
BUT I STAND IN CONTROLLED
I STAND ALONE
BUT I STAND FREE

Mi Changa

My Monkey, mi changita
Yes, my monkey
Making me laugh, hurt, and flustered
Si, tu eres mi changita (Yes, you are my little monkey)
Making me itch, scratch and claw
Yes, my monkey, mi changita linda (my cute little monkey)
Making me feel loved
Yes, through feedings
Through our talks
Yes, through touches and hugs
Tu eres mi changita chula (You are my cute little monkey)
And NO
DON'T GO!!!!!

Mother to Son

Life's not been one of fun and games
'specially one of many
Sixteen on the exacta
Post W.W. I and pre-W.W. II
Reconstructing if not rebuilding homes, family and friends
Unknowing the face of breakfast, lunch or dinner
Sleeping in alleys, trucks or depots
Still together, still united
Lincoln poor but love endowed
Crossing borders, tongues and cultures
Draining, struggling, and searching
Clouded dreams, obtainable goals
Now, clothed, fed, sheltered and loved
Until death do us part . . .

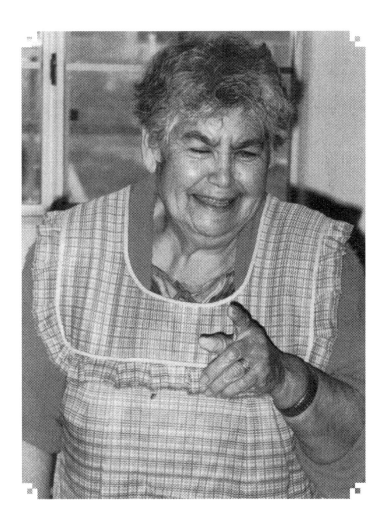

My brothers-in-arms

He answered to one
Productive, rugged or leathered
He answered to one
Seeing persistence and humor
He answered to one
Signally loyalty, honor and joy
He answered to one
Robbed of youth, rebellion soared
He answered to one

My Path

My path . . .
Obscured yet deliberate
My path . . .
Independent yet dependent
My path . . .
Empty yet unsettling
My path . . .
Disarrayed yet opportunistic
My path . . .
Questioned yet answered

No more

Exposed & Uncovered
No more . . .
Ignored beaten & injured
No more . . .
Self-esteem *ridiculed*
No more . . .
Seeking friendship
No more . . .
Seeking worth
No more . . .
Desiring needs
No more . . .
Desiring wants
No more . . .
I would play no more
*I will cry **no more***
No more . . . No more

Now...

You **welcomed**
I **ignored**
You **warned**
I disregarded
You *created*
I *destroyed*
You *carried*
I ***crushed***
You ***embraced***
Openly and willingly
Easing discomfort, easing pain
Forgiving *forgetting*
*Now, I **embrace***
Now, ***I praise***
Now, *I love*

Once Upon a Time

PD - POWERFUL & DANGEROUS
ONCE UPON A TIME . . .
HG - HONEST & GENUINE
ONCE UPON A TIME . . .
LEAVING NO REGRETS
ONCE UPON A TIME . . .
KEEPING TRUE TO ONE'S SELF
ONCE UPON A TIME . . .
WHILE IGNITING THE FIRE WITHIN
ONCE UPON A TIME . . .
SEIZING THE MOMENT
ONCE UPON A TIME . . .
STRONG, FREE & SHIELDED
ONCE UPON A TIME . . .
THINKING OF YOU, THINKING OF ME
ONCE UPON A TIME . . .
YOU ARE THE ONLY ONE
ONCE UPON A TIME . . .

The Other Way...

Common was her look
the other way...
Hypnotic was her glare
the other way...
Entangled by her web
the other way...
Choked by her heart
the other way...
Hungered for a touch
the other way...
Pained by the kiss withheld
the other way...
Rejected by nonexistence
the other way...
Death caused by friendship
the other way...

Over the rainbow

One dreams high
Over the rainbow . . .
Wishing, melting, flying
Over the rainbow . . .
True dreams sweeten or sour
Over the rainbow . . .
Stars wake, sleep all around or die
Over the rainbow . . .
While clouds behind "DREAM" that DARE
Over the rainbow . . .
What a Wonder – this WORLD
Over the rainbow . . .
Seeing, thinking, growing, watching, and learning
Over the rainbow . . .

Passage…

Strangers passing
Boats colliding
Ships eluding
Tranquil peace
Silent waters
Fiery beauty
Unforgiven revelations
Blinded journey
Unanswered queries
Transparent visions
Visible markers
Stepping forward
Stepping back

Philanthropist

A giver
Touching all around
Some by green
Others ridin' the emotional wave
Receiving
Giving
Asking why
Replying,
"We can, because we are"

Promised…

A second, a minute, an hour
PROMISED . . .
A time or a place
Go-carts, beaches, sunsets or juices
PROMISED . . .
That timeless smile, laugh, or look
Beauty & the beast
PROMISED . . .
Planned, scheduled or unrehearsed
Memories past, present and tomorrow
Special, unique, and reserved
PROMISED . . .
Together, promised, engaged, and wedded
Supportive, combative, and resolved
Combined, united, one

Reach Out...

Just out of reach . . .
The stars, the moon
Just out of reach . . .
The shadows of fear
Just out of reach . . .
The grin, the smile
Just out of reach . . .
The light, the look
The touch, the hold
The tender lips, the missing kiss
Just out of reach . . .
My friend, my lady
Just out of reach . . .

Renaissance

Exposed & uncovered *for who I was*
Later ignored BEATEN & INJURED
My self-esteem *ridiculed*
Seeking FRIENDSHIP
Seeking worth
Desiring NEEDS
Desiring wants
Dancing realized no more
Flying grasped no more
No more . . . No more

Ripped, torn and shredded

My knight in armor
His anticipated smile - My day
His embrace - My heart
His arrogance - My mistrust
His deceit - My care
His lies - My faith
Ripped, torn & shredded
I gave him away
Ripped, torn & shredded

Road Rage

Driving, pacing, racing
Lane changes, cutoffs, and brake lights
Street Lights - Green-Go, Yellow-Caution
the almighty Red
Stop! Stop!! Crash!!!
Street signs – signaling turns, pending curves
Ignoring exits, one-ways, or dead ends
Road Rage - interest controlled
Lost, lost, lost

Robbed Chances

Thinking young
Thinking color
ROBBED CHANCES . . .
Universal racism
Discriminatory tolerance
ROBBED CHANCES . . .
Recalling oppressed blind pain
Preventing liberties
ROBBED CHANCES . . .
Substandard ideology
Dollars over humanity
ROBBED CHANCES . . .
Surfacing equality through prosperity
Poverty's awaiting resurrection
ROBBED CHANCES . . .

Sunrise Sunset

Sunrise Sunset
We Meet Again
Mother & Father
Creator of life
We Meet Again
Brothers and Sister
Argue, quarrel and fight
We Meet Again
Young, old and in-between
Leaving, returning and departing
We Meet Again
Experienced, learned, and educated
Growing, maturing, gaining admiration, respect, and loyalty
We Meet Again
Building stories, tales, and memories
Good or bad but created
We Meet Again
Yesterday, today or tomorrow
Eating, drinking or resting
We Meet Again
Journey East, West, North or South
Traveling in peace, harmony and strength
We meet again

Sweet, sweet dreams

I want to be there . . .
To hold you
To miss you
I want to be there . . .
To kiss you
To love you
I want to be there . . .
To say, "My shining star"
To say, "My inspiration"
I want to be there . . .
Your special care
Your special stare
I want to be there . . .
Tender touches,
Tender feels,
Tender whispers,
"Good night, sweet dreams"
I want to be there . . .

To Die For…

Alone but loved
To die for . . .
Sacrificing ONE
Sacrificing I
To die for . . .
Seeking TRUTH
Seeking SATISFACTION
To die for . . .
Selfish but GIVING
To die for . . .
This BLACK ROSE
This BEAUTY
This DIAMOND
This PEARL
To die for . . .

Unfinished business

Yesterday, today or tomorrow
We regress
Wishing, wanting, or needing
We regress
The thought, the act, the moment
We regress
The unknown if not the unrecognized
We regress
A stranger without a name, a family or meaning
We regress
Ignoring a glance, a look, a word
We regress
Continuing the game or the play
We regress
Yielding sins and removing wonders
We regress
Business undone

Unrecognized...

Individual inadequacies
Unrecognized *Undefined*...
Unmeasureable powers
Unrecognized *Undefined*...
Illuminating fear over frightened darkness
Unrecognized *Undefined*...
Humility over arrogance and conceit
Unrecognized *Undefined*...
Acceptance over concealed talent
Unrecognized *Undefined*...
Liberated fear liberated followers
Unrecognized *Undefined*...
Insecurities...
Recognized, Recognized, Recognized...

The Way You Are...

I want you
The way you are
The real not false
The way you are
No turning, adjusting, or fine tuning
The way you are
Not changed, not altered
The way you are
Stay this way not that
The way you are
Today's not yesterday's or tomorrow's you
The way you are
What I would want
The way you are
Not need
The way you are

We...

Finding COMMON INTEREST
We . . .
Needed EXECUTion
We . . .
Setting GOALs
We . . .
PREPARing ourselves
We . . .
LEARNing that TEAM has no I
We . . .
BONDing, COOPERATing & UNITing
We . . .
CONNECTing,
We . . .
LISTENing to UNDERSTANDing
We . . .
And KNOWing
We . . .
FOCUSing
We . . .
SEEing & DIRECTing
We . . .
BELIEVing
We . . .
ASSISTing

And CELEBRATing
We . . .
BECOMing ONE
We . . .
NEEDing a BEGINning
A PATH, a GOAL, a FOCUS
We . . .
PREPARing ourselves
Through SUPPORT, COOPERATION, & UNITY
We . . .
NEEDing to be ONE, to CONNECT, to LEAD
We . . .
LISTENing, UNDERSTANDing, SEEing
We . . .
KNOWing our place
BEGINning EXECUTION
PROVIDing DIRECTION and ASSISTANCE
We . . .
PROVIDing BELIEF
ASSISTANCE and CELEBRATION
We . . .
You and I . . .

What if...

What if. . .
I had left you
Would my life have purpose
Would it have meaning
What if. . .
We would have never met
Would we be where we are
What if. . .
I had asked
And you had agreed
What if. . .
I would have tried
Would your back be turned
What if. . .
I say, "You are my
Juliet, my day, my night,
my everything."
What if. . .
I'll always care
What if. . .
I'll always love you
What if. . .

When I go

When I go to the great beyond
How will you remember me?
As a person of meanness
As a person that is crazed
Or one that you laughed, cried and 'chilled' with
When I go will you think of me?
Or will you forget me?
Will you remember the ups and downs?
The good and the bad
Or will you erase the memories of me?
When I go, will you miss me?
Or will you forget I ever existed?
When I go, will you still love me as if I was around?
Or will you forget that you loved me?
Or will you be happy for me, that I feel no pain?
And I've gone to a better place?
When I go I ask one thing of you?
Remember who I was to you
Brother, sister, spouse, parent, or grandparent
When I go

You Are My Luster, My Glow

Defending its physicality through thorns
Or hiding its pain
Awaking its yellowish tint for an I care vision
Or blooming white its innocence
While yielding orange colored fascination and enthusiasm
Or reveal its beauty and perfection through its redness
Yet providing a single sign of devotion
Or holding a hidden 13 for admiration
Yes, my special pedal
Yes, my special lady
Yes, my rose
My Lona Chameli

Youths of Today

Looked at
With smiles or sadness
Youths of today
Soap operas maturation or explosions
Occurring events here and there
Youths of today
Presenting evil hearts
Or one's love or forgiveness
The youth of today
Everything right
Timing wrong
Youths of today
Fiery relationships
Changing opinions
These youths of today,
Tomorrow, or yesteryear

LIFE

Experiences
TALES
Actions
ARE
Their interpretations
ORDERED
They are the dealings
BY
Reached agreements
ME
Delivered arrangements
MYSELF
Signed pacts
AND I

Thank you for lending me your eyes to read, your time to digest, and your mind to decipher my lines. I hope you enjoyed them.

Printed in the United States
By Bookmasters